Perfect Pictures Stories

For
Language Learning

By

Lonnie Dai Zovi

Artwork by James Perry III

Vibrante Press
Albuquerque, N.M.

Perfect Pictures Stories

For
Language Learning

By

Lonnie Dai Zovi

Artwork by James Perry III

ISBN13 – 0-935301-82-3

Vibrante Press
P.O.Box 51853
Albuquerque, N.M.
87181

Perfect Pictures Stories

For
Language Learning

As a language teacher, you know that pictures in the language classroom are a necessary part of your teaching materials. Pictures can explain or elicit what mere words or actions cannot. This collection of sequential pictures is meant to augment your integrated program of language development. They can be used for listening comprehension, TPRS (Teaching Reading Through Reading and Storytelling), speaking practice, dialogue or play suggestions, or writing practice. Because the stories are divided into six frames, they closely resemble the Advanced Placement format and therefore make an excellent practice for this test as well. The stories are not arranged in any specific order so they may be used as thematic supplements (for example using Picture Story 1 when weather is being studied) or simply use the stories as a weekly or otherwise sequential speaking or writing activity. The *Picture Stories Vocabulary and Questions* before each story is meant to be a speaking or writing stimulus. Of course you may choose not to use the vocabulary and have the students use your suggested vocabulary or use their own dictionaries.

Speaking Practice – Pass out the Picture Story. Write on the board the suggested vocabulary and discuss the meanings if necessary. Of course you may want to add. Delete or change some words to your dialectical or other preference. As a large group or in small groups, have the students talk about the pictures. If the class n

eeds extra stimulus, you may want to use the questions provided/

TPRS Stories – All of these stories lend themselves well to stories for TRPS stories. If you are not familiar with the methodology, you might want to go to look it up on the web or go to www.blaineraytprs.com to find out more.

Writing Practice – There are many ways to use these pictures for writing practice, a few of which are mentioned here. As a prelude to better writing, you need to make sure that the key vocabulary is learned. It is a good idea to first do simple listening and speaking activities. After that you might want the students to write a list of possible nouns, verbs, adjectives, adverbs, transitional words and others that could be used for more colorful and interesting writing. You could specify which tense you want used, if you want dialogues or not, how many adjectives you want, how many words you want. (Example, perhaps the first story you will only say that you want 100 words. The next 150 words, but with at least 3 adjectives. The third can have 3 adverbs, the forth 3 adjectives plus 3 adverbs, and so on.) If time permits, you can have the stories peer edited for mistakes and/or understandability. You can read the stories aloud, but only the most interesting. I find that the students try harder if there is a chance that their stories might be picked. You could even have a contest to see which is the most interesting. Hopefully the students will rewrite the stories so that they may learn from their mistakes.

Plays – Act these stories out, memorized or not. They'll love it. Film them and show it to the parents! Have fun while learning.

Picture Stories

Perfect Picture Stories

English - 1

sun –
sunglasses –
it's sunny –
it's raining –
lightning –
umbrella -

It's snowing -
Snowman -
cap -
scarf -
jacket -
melts -

1. Who is in the room?
2. What is he doing?
3. What does he see?
4. What does he want to do?
5. What does he need?
6. What does he wear outside?
7. What happens now that he's outside?
8. Why does he return inside?
9. What does he get?
10. Where does he put his sunglasses?

11. What does he see outside?
12. Is he well dressed for the weather?
13. Why does he go back inside?
14. How does he dress now?
15. What doesn't he see in the window?
16. What does he see outside?
17. What is he thinking?
18. What is he going to do now?

Français 1

soleil
lunettes de soleil
il fait soleil
il pleut
éclairs
parapluie

il neige
bonhomme de neige
casquette
écharpe
veste
fondre

1. Qui est dans la pièce?
2. Que fait-il?
3. Que voit-il ?
4. Que veut-il faire?
5. De quoi a-t-il besoin?
6. Que porte-t-il dehors?
7. Qu'est-ce qui se passe maintenant
   qu'il est dehors?
8. Pourquoi rentre-t-il?
9. Que prend-il?
10. Où mets-il ses lunettes de soleil?

11. Que voit-il dehors?
12. Est-il bien habillé pour le temps
    qu'il fair?
13. Pourquoi rentre-t-il ?
14. Comment s'habille-t-il maintenant?
15. Qu'est ce qu'il ne voit pas par la
    fenêtre?
16. Que voit-il dehors?
17. Que pense-t-il?
18. Que va-t-il faire maintenant?

Español - 1

sol –
anteojos de sol –
hace sol –
está lloviendo –
relámpago –
paraguas -

está nevando-
mono de nieve -
gorra -
bufanda -
chaqueta -
derretirse (i) –

1. ¿Quién está en el cuarto?
2. ¿Qué está haciendo?
3. ¿Qué ve él?
4. ¿Qué quiere hacer?
5. ¿Qué necesita?
6. ¿Qué lleva puesto afuera?
7. ¿Qué pasa afuera ahora?
8. ¿Por qué regresa adentro?
9. ¿Qué necesita ahora?

10. ¿Dónde pone sus anteojos de sol?
11. ¿Qué pasa afuera?
12. ¿Está bien vestido para el tiempo?
13. ¿Por qué regresa afuera?
14. ¿Ahora cómo se viste?
15. ¿Qué no ve por la ventana?
16. ¿Qué ve afuera esta vez?
17. ¿Qué estará pensando?
18. ¿Qué decide hacer después?

Perfect Picture Stories

English- 2

leave –
rug –
lamp –
couch –
garbage –
box –
empty –

key –
climb –
dot –
walls –
striped –
mess –
wrong –

1. Where is the woman now?
2. Where is she going?
3. What does her living room look like?
4. What does she see as she goes outside?
5. What is next to the garbage can?
6. Upon returning, what does she do?
7. What is the problem?
8. What does she need to do now?
9. How will she enter her locked house?
10. What does she use to help her enter?
11. What does she see in the house?
12. What is she thinking?
13. What is the cat thinking?
14. What does she notice outside?
15. What is the address?
16. What is her address?
17. Why did she make this mistake?
18. Who is the man in the car?

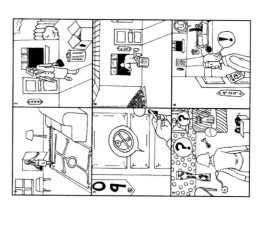

Français 2

laisser
tapis
lampe
canapé
poubelle
boîte
vide

clef
grimper
point
murs
rayé
desordre
faux

1. Où est la femme maintenant?
2. Où va-t-elle?
3. Comment est son salon?
4. Que voit-elle lorsqu'elle sort?
5. Pourquoi y-a-t-il une boîte près de la poubelle?
6. Qu'essaie-t-elle de faire lorsqu'elle revient?
7. Quel estle problème?
8. Que doit-elle faire maintenant?
9. Comment va-t-elle entrer dans sa maison?
10. De quoi s'aide-t-elle pour entrer?
11. Que voit-elle dans la maison?
12. Que pense-t-elle?
13. Que pense le chat?
14. Que remarque-t-elle dehors?
15. Quelle est l'adresse de cette maison?
16. Quelle est son adresse à elle?
17. Pourrquoi a-t-elle fâir cet erreur?
18. Qui est l'homme dans la voiture?

Español - 2

salir -
alfombra –
lámpara –
sofá –
basura –
caja –
vacío -

llave -
trepar -
punto -
paredes -
rayado -
desórden -
equivocado –

1. ¿Dónde está la mujer?
2. ¿Adónde va?
3. Describe su sala.
4. ¿Qué ve antes de irse?
5. ¿Por qué hay una caja afuera?
6. ¿Qué trata de hacer al regresar?
7. ¿Cuál es el problema?
8. ¿Qué necesita hacer ahora?
9. ¿Cómo entra a la casa?
10. ¿Qué ve una vez adentro?
11. ¿Qué pensará?
12. ¿Qué mira afuera?
13. ¿Cuál es la dirección de la casa?
14. ¿Cuál es su dirección?
15. ¿Cómo se equivocó?
16. ¿Quién pasa en su carro?

Picture Story 2

Perfect Picture Stories

English - 3

menu –
tablecloth –
waiter –
napkin –
chicken

order -
delicious -
fishing -
chef -
kitchen --

1. Where is the family?
2. Who else is at the restaurant?
3. What are they doing?
4. Who approaches the table?
5. What does he ask the man?
6. What does the man order?
7. What does the cook tell the waiter?
8. What does he tell his customer?
9. Now what does the man order?

10. What is his son doing?
11. Why isn't he sitting down?
12. What is the man thinking?
13. Do they have fish ?
14. What do the cook and waiter do?
15. Why do they do that?
16. Is that a good idea?
17. Will the customer be happy?
18. Will it take a long time?

Español - 3

menú –
mantel –
mesero -
servilleta –
cocinero -

pollo-
cocina -
pedir -
sabroso -
pescar –

1. ¿Dónde está la familia?
2. ¿Quién más está allí?
3. ¿Qué están haciendo?
4. ¿Quién se acerca a la mesa?
5. ¿Qué le pregunta al hombre?
6. ¿Qué pide el señor?
7. ¿Qué dice el cocinero?
8. ¿Qué le dice el mesero al señor?
9. Entonces, ¿ qué pide él?

10. ¿Qué hace el hijo?
11. ¿Por qué no se sienta?
12. ¿Qué piensa el papá?
13. ¿Tienen pescado?
14. ¿Qué hacen afuera?
15. ¿Por qué?
16. ¿Es buena idea?
17. ¿Estará feliz el cliente?
18. ¿Tardará mucho tiempo?

Français 3

menu
nappe
serveur
serviette
poulet

commande
délicieux
pêcher
chef
cuisine

1. Où est la famille?
2. Qui d'autre est au restaurant?
3. Que font-ils?
4. Qui s'approche de la table?
5. Que demande-t-il a l'homme?
6. Que commande l'homme?
7. Que dit le cuisinier au serveur?
8. Que dit le serveur au client?
9. Maintenant, que commande le client?

10. Que fait le fils?
11. Pourquoi n'est-il pas bien assis?
12. Que pense l'homme?
13. Ont-ils du poisson?
14. Que font le cuisinier et le serveur?
15. Pourquoi font-ils cela?
16. Est-ce une bonne idée?
17. Le client sera-t-il content?
18. Est-ce-que cela va prendre beaucoup de temps?

Picture Story 3

Perfect Picture Stories

English – 4

underdeveloped –
hut –
missionaries –
primitive –
light bulb –
suitcase –
to board -

1. Where are the people?
2. Who is talking?
3. What is he saying?
4. Who are the people?
5. What do they pack in a box?
6. Why do they pack these things?
7. Where are they going?
8. How are they going to get there?
9. What do they bring with them?

canoe -
crocodile -
snakes -
jungle –
to float –
dangerous –
electricity -

10. When they land what do they do?
11. What do they see in the water?
12. What kind of place are they in?
13. What is one of the boys doing?
14. What does the village look like?
15. Is this what they expected?
16. What do they see in the huts?
17. Is this what they expected to see?
18. How is this possible?

Français 4

sous-dévellopé
case
missionaires
primitif
ampoule électrique
valise
embarquer

1. Qui sont les gens?
2. Qui parle?
3. Que dit-il?
4. Qui sont les personnes?
5. Qu'emballent-ils dans la boîte?
6. Pourquoi emballent-ils ces choses?
7. Où vont-ils?
8. Comment vont-ils y aller ?
9. Qu'amenent-ils avec eux?

canoë
crocodile
serpents
jungle
flotter
dangéreux
électricité

10. Que font-ils quand ils atterrissent?
11. Que voient-ils dans l'eau?
12. Dans quelle sorte d'endroit sont-ils?
13. Que fait l'un des garçons?
14. Décrivez le village?
15. C'est à cela ce qu'ils s'attendaient?
16. Que voient-ils dans les cases?
17. Est-ce ce qu'ils s'attendaient a voir?
18. Comment est-ce possible?

Español - 4

primitivo –
choza –
misioneros –
foco –
maleta -
embarcar -

1. ¿Dónde están las personas?
2. ¿Quién habla?
3. ¿Qué dice?
4. ¿Quiénes son los otros?
5. ¿Qué empacan en las cajas?
6. ¿Por qué?
7. ¿Adónde irán ellos?
8. ¿Cómo irán?
9. ¿Qué traen con ellos?

canoa -
cocodrilo -
serpientes-
selva -
peligroso -
electricidad –

10. ¿Qué hacen al aterrizar?
11. ¿Qué ven en el agua?
12. ¿En qué tipo de lugar están?
13. Describe la aldea.
14. ¿Qué hace uno de los niños?
15. ¿Es esto lo que esperaban?
16. ¿Qué ven en las chozas?
17. ¿ Qué habían esperado ver?
18. ¿Cómo es posible todo esto?

Picture Story 4

Perfect Picture Stories

Français 5

se détendre
gratter
maître
attirer l'attention
collier
laisse
clown
emmener pour une promenade

laisser aller
poursuivre
portier
portes tournantes
s'aggripper à
trottoir
ballons

1.Où est le jeune homme?
2.Que fait-il?
3.Que veut le chien?
4.Comment attire-t-il l'attention de son maître?
5.Où est-ce-que le maître amène le chien?
6.Sont-ils en ville ou à la campagne?
7.Qu'est-ce-que le maître mets autour du cou de son chien?
8.Qui rencontre-t-il dans la rue?
9.De quoi parlent-ils?

10.Que tient-elle dans ses bras?
11.Qu'essaie de faire le chien?
12.Qu'arrive-t-il au chat?
13.Où court le chat?
14.Que fait le chien?
15.Que fait le jeune homme?
16.Que fait la jeune femme?
17.Qu'arrive-t-il a tout le monde?
18. Lres deux, vont-ils rester ami

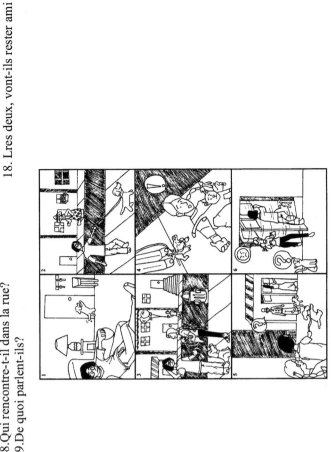

English – 5

relax –
scratching –
master–
get attention –
collar –
leash –
clown –
take for a walk –

let go -
chase -
bell-hop-
revolving door -
hold on -
balloons -
sidewalk -

1. Where is the young man?
2. What is he doing?
3. What does the dog want?
4. How does he get his master's attention?
5. What does the owner put on the dog?
6. Are they in the city or the country?
7. Where does the owner take his dog?
8. Who does he meet in the street?
9. What do they talk about?

10. What does she have in her arms?
11. What does the dog try to do?
12. What happens to the cat?
13. Where does the cat run?
14. What does the dog do?
15. What does the young man do?
16. What does the young woman do?
17. What happens to everybody?
18. Will the two people stay friends?

Español - 5

relajar –
rascando –
el amo –
llamar la atención –
collar –
correa –
payaso –
pasear –

acera -
globos -
soltar -
perseguir -
botones -
puerta giradora -
agarrar -

1. ¿Dónde está el joven?
2. ¿Qué hace?
3. ¿Qué quiere el perro?
4. ¿Cómo llama su atención?
5. ¿Adónde le lleva el amo?
6. ¿Están en el campo o la ciudad?
7. ¿Qué le pone al pescuezo?
8. ¿A quién encuentra en la calle?
9. ¿De qué hablan?

10. ¿Qué tiene en sus brazos?
11. ¿Qué trate de hacer el perro?
12. ¿Qué le pasa al gato?
13. ¿Hacia dónde corre el gato?
14. ¿Qué hace el perro?
15. ¿Qué hace el joven?
16. ¿Qué hace la joven?
17. Al final,¿qué les pasa?
18. ¿Seguirán siendo amigos los dos?

Picture Story 5

Perfect Picture Stories

English - 6

cane –
vacation –
skiing –
skateboarding –
mountain climbing –
excited –
anticipating –
run into –
pole –
pine tree –

manhole –
helmet -
trip -
rock -
bump -
sling -
cast -
crutches -
bandage -
limping -

1. Where are these people?
2. Who are these people?
3. What are they discussing?
4. What are the students planning ?
5. How do they feel about it?
6. What happens to the first young man?
7. How did it happen?
8. What happens to the other young man?
9. Why did it happen?
10. What happened to the girl?
11. Where was she?
12. What was she doing and why?
13. How do the three return to class?
14. What does the teacher say?
15. How do they answer her ?
16. What lessons did they learn?

Français 6

canne
vacances
faire du ski
patiner à la planch à roulettes
escalade
egité
anticiper
enfocer
bâton
pin

bouche d'egout
casque
voyage
rocher
frapper,heurter
écharpe
plâtre
béquilles
bandage
boîter

1. Où sont ces gens?
2. Qui sont ces gens?
3. De quoi parlent-ils?
4. Qu'organisent les élèves?
5. Qu'en penset-ils?
6. Qu'arrive-t-il au premier jeune homme?
7. Comment est-ce que cela arrive?
8. Qu'arrive-t-il au deuxième jeune homme?
9. Pourquoi est-ce que cela arrive?
10. Qu'est-il arrive à la fille?
11. Où était-elle?
12. Que faisait-elle et pourquoi?
13. Comment les 3 élèves retournent-ils en classe?
14. Que dit le professeur?
15. Que lui repondent-ils?
16. Quelle leçon en ont-ils tiré?

Español - 6

bastón –
casco -
esquiar –
andar en patineta –
escalar –
chocar –
escarpas -

agujero -
pegar -
piedra -
yeso -
muletas -
ventajas -
cojear -

1. ¿Dónde están ellos?
2. ¿De qué hablan?
3. ¿Cuáles son sus planes?
4. ¿Cómo se sienten hoy?
5. ¿Qué le pasa al primero?
6. ¿Qué le pasa al otro?
7. ¿Por qué les pasó?
8. ¿Qué le pasó a la joven?
9. ¿Dónde estaba?
10. ¿Qué estaba haciendo?
11. ¿Cómo regresaron a clase?
12. ¿Qué les dijo la maestra?
13. ¿Qué les contestó?
14. ¿Cuál fue la lección aprendida?

Picture Story 6

Perfect Picture Stories

English - 7

classmate —
invite —
accept —
a dance —
suit —
a tie —
try on —
fit -

mirror -
price tag -
spill -
stain -
snack -
washing machine -
shrink -
horrified —

1. Where do the two people talk?
2. About what time of day is it?
3. What does the boy ask the girl?
4. Does she want to go?
5. What does the boy do now?
6. What kind of store is it?
7. What is in the store specifically?
8. What might the salesclerk and the boy be talking about?

9. What does he do when he gets home?
10. What does he do in the kitchen?
11. How does he feel about this?
12. Where does he go now?
13. Why does he go there?
14. What happens to his suit?
15. What is he going to do now?

\ Français 7

camarade de classe
inviter
accepter
bal
costume
cravate
essayer
horrifié

miroir
étiquette
renverser
tache
casse-croûte
machine à laveré
retrecir

1. Où parlent-ils, les deux personnes?
2. Quelle heure est-il plus ou moins?
3. Que demande le jeune homme à la jeune fille?
4. Veut-elle y aller?
5. Que fait le garçon maintenant?
6. Quelle sorte de magasin est-ce?
7. Qu'est-ce qu'il y a de spécial dans le magasin?
8. De quoi est-ce-que le vendeur et le garçon sont probablement en train de parler?

9. Que fait-il quand il arrive à la maisc
10. Qu fait-il dans la cuisine?
11. Qu'en pense-t-il?
12. Ou va-t-il maintenant?
13. Pourquoi va-t-il la-bas?
14. Qu'arrive-t-il a son costume?
15. Que va-t-il faire maintenant?

Español - 7

compañero —
invitar —
aceptar —
un baile —
corbata —
probarse —
quedarse bien -
traje -

espejo -
etiqueta -
derramar -
manchar -
bocado -
lavadora -
encogerse -
pasmado —

1. ¿Dónde hablan los jovenes?
2. ¿Qué hora será?
3. ¿Qué le dice el joven?
4. ¿Qué le contesta?
5. ¿Ahora qué hace el joven?
6. ¿Qué tipo de tienda es?
7. Específicamente¿qué hay allí?
8. ¿Qué le dice el dependiente?

9. ¿Qué hace al regresar a casa?
10. ¿Qué hace en la cocina?
11. ¿Cómo reacciona?
12. ¿Adónde va a ahora?
13. ¿Por qué?
14. ¿Qué le pasa a su traje?
15. ¿Qué va a pasar ahora?
16. ¿Qué harías tú?

Perfect Picture Stories

English – 8

wig –
bald –
date –
bouquet –
elegant –
candlelight –

1. What is the woman doing?
2. Why is she doing that?
3. What does she look like?
4. Why does she look like this?
5. Who comes to her door?
6. What does he look like?
7. What does she look like now?
8. Where do they go and why?

9. Where do they walk?
10. What things do they see?
11. What time of day is it?
12. What does the seagull do?
13. What does she do now?
14. What does he do?
15. Will they still to be friends?
16. What would you do in this case?

Español - 8

peluca –
calvo –
cita –
ramo –
elegante –
velas -

1. ¿Qué hace la mujer?
2. ¿Por qué?
3. Descríbela.
4. ¿Por qué se parece así?
5. ¿Quién viene a la puerta?
6. Descríbelo.
7. Descríbela ahora.
8. ¿Adónde van y por qué?

9. ¿Por dónde caminan?
10. ¿Qué cosas ven allí?
11. ¿Qué hora será?
12. ¿Qué hace la gaviota?
13. ¿Qué hace la mujer?
14. ¿Qué hace el hombre?
15. ¿Seguirán siendo amigos?

playa -
gaviota -
cangrejo-
agarrar -
perseguir -
avergonzado –

Français 8

perruque
chauve
rendez-vous
bouquet
élégant
lumière chandelle

1. Que fait la femme?
2. Pourquoi fait-elle cela?
3. Que ressemble-t-elle?
4. Pourquoi a-t-elle l'air comme cela?
5. Qui vient à sa porte?
6. De quoi a-t-il l'air?

7. De quoi a-t-elle l'air maintenant?
8. Où vont-ils et pourquoi?

plage
mouette
crabe
attrapper
poursuivre
embarrassé

9. Où se promènent-ils?
10. Quelles choses voient-ils?
11. Quelle heure est-il?
12. Que fait la mouette?
13. Que fait la femme?
14. Que fait son copain (petit ami)?
15. Vont-ils rester amis?

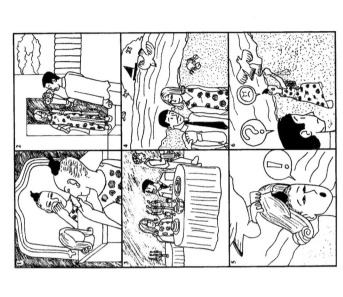

beach –
seagull -
crab -
grab -
chase -
embarrassed –

Perfect Picture Stories

English - 9

businessman –
notes –
train station –
train tracks –
operating –
engineer –
on time –

bridge –
traffic –
taxi –
in a hurry –
bicyclist –
speech –

1. Where is the businessman?
2. What is he on the way to do?
3. What does he have in his hands?
4. How is he going to get there?
5. What does he see there?
6. Will it be fixed anytime soon?
7. How does he feel?
8. Now how is he going to get there?

9. What is the problem?
10. Now what does he see?
11. What does he want from the boy?
12. Why?
13. What does he offer him?
14. Does he make it to meeting?
15. Is he on time?
16. Do you think he was a success?

Español - 9

hombre de negocio –
apuntes –
estación de tren –
las vías –
operar –
ingeniero –
a tiempo -

puente -
tráfico -
taxi -
de prisa -
biciclista -
discurso -

1. ¿Dónde está el caballero?
2. ¿Qué va a hacer hoy?
3. ¿Qué tiene en las manos?
4. ¿Cómo había querido viajar?
5. ¿Qué es lo que ve una vez allí?
6. ¿Podrán componerlo pronto?
7. ¿Cómo se siente?
8. ¿Ahora cómo piensa viajar?

9. ¿Cuál es el problema?
10. Ahora ¿qué es lo que ve?
11. ¿Qué quiere del chico?
12. ¿Por qué?
13. ¿Qué le ofrece?
14. ¿Llega a la reunión?
15. ¿Llega a tiempo?
16. ¿Tuvo éxito?

Français 9

homme d'affaires
notes
gare
rail
faire marcher
ingeniéur
à l'heure

pont
cirulation
taxi
êpressé
cycliste
discours

1. Où est l'homme?
2. Qu'est-ce qu'il est en train de faire?
3. Que tient-il dans ses mains?
4. Comment va-t-il arriver à destination?
5. Qu'est-ce qu'il y voit?
6. Est-ce-que cela sera bientôt réparé?
7. Comment se sent-il?
8. Maintenant, comment va-t-il aller?

9. Quel est le probleme?
10. Que voit-il maintenant?
11. Que veux-t-il du garçon?
12. Pourquoi?
13. Que lui offre-t-il?
14. Arrive-t-il à sa reunion?
15. Est-il à l'heure?
16. Pensez vous qu'il a fait un succès?

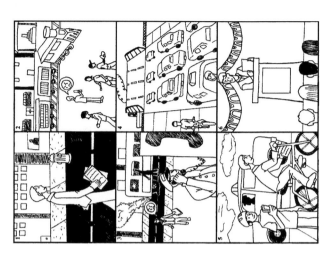

Picture Story 9

Perfect Picture Stories

English - 10

cling onto –
stubborn –
refuse –
building blocks –
toys –

playmates -
playground -
fun -
crying –
surprised –

1. What room of the house are they in?
2. What are they doing?
3. What time of year is this?
4. Where is he going?
5. How does the boy feel about this?
6. How does the mother feel?
7. What does he do with the blocks?
8. Is he playing alone with the blocks?

9. What does he do?
10. Is he having fun?
11. What's outside?
12. What are they playing ?
13. What happens after school?
14. What does the boy do?
15. Why?
16. How does the mother react?

Español - 10

no soltar –
testarudo –
rehusar –
bloques –
juguetes -

compañeros -
terreno par jugar -
diversión -
llorando -
sorprendido -

1. ¿En cuál cuarto están?
2. ¿!ué están haciendo?
3. ¿Qué estación es?
4. ¿Adónde va?
5. ¿Cómo se siente?
6. ¿Cómo se siente la mamá?
7. ¿Qué hace con los bloques?
8. ¿Juega solo?

9. ¿Qué hace con los niños?
10. ¿Se divierte mucho?
11. ¿Qué hay afuera?
12. ¿Qué hacen allí?
13. ¿Qué pasa después de clases?
14. ¿Qué hace el niño?
15. ¿Por qué?
16. ¿Cómo reacciona la mamá?

Français 10

se cramponner à
entêté
refuser
jeu de bâtiment
jouets

un ami
cour de récréation
amusement
pleurer
surpris

1. Dans quelle pièce de la maison se
trouvent-ils?
2. Que font-ils?
3. Quelle saison de l'année est-ce?
4. Où va-t-il?
5. Qu'en pense le garçon?
6. Qu'en pense la mère?
7. Que fait-il avec le jeu de
bâtiment?
8. Joue-t-il seul avec le jeu de bâtiment?

9. Que fait-il avec les enfants?
10. S'amuse-t-il?
11. Qu'est-ce qu'il y a dehors?
12. A quoi jouent-ils dehors?
13. Que se passe-t-il après l'école?
14. Que fait le garçon?
15. Pourquoi?
16. Comment réagit la mère?

Picture Story 10

Perfect Picture Stories

Français 11

shopping — marché
stand
montrer du doigt
panier
cuisine
peler
peau

arranger
figure
pleurer
poire
orange
banane
raisin
assiette

1. Où vont la mère et la fille?
2. Que voit la fille?
3. Que veut-elle que sa mère achète?
4. Y a-t-il beaucoup de monde?
5. Où va la fille quand elle arrive à la maison?
6. Où ont-ils mis le fruit?
7. Est-ce que sa maison est moderne ou à l'ancienne mode?
8. Comment le sait-on?
9. Qu'est que la fille ouvre?
10. Que sort-elle?
11. Pourquoi en a-t-elle besoin?
12. Que fait-elle?
13. Qu'a-t-elle mis sur l'assiette?
14. Qu'a-t-elle utilisé pour les yeux?
15. Qu'a-t-elle utilisé pour le nez?
16. Quoi d'autre a-t-ell utilisé?

English - 11

shopping —
market —
stalls —
pointing —
basket —
kitchen —
peel —
skin —

arrange -
face -
crying -
pear -
orange -
bananas -
grapes -
plate —

1. Where do the mother and daughter go?
2. What does the daughter see?
3. What does she want her mother to buy?
4. Are there very many people there?
5. Where does the girl go?
6. Where have they put the fruit?
7. Is her house modern or old-fashioned?
8. How do you know?
9. What does the girl open?
10. What does she take out?
11. Why does she need it?
12. What is she doing?
13. What's on the plate?
14. What's used for eyes?
15. What's used for a nose?
16. What else has she used?

Español - 11

compras —
mercado —
puesto —
apuntando —
canasta —
cocina —
pelar —
cáscara —

acomodar -
cara -
pera -
naranja -
plátanos -
uvas -
plato -

1. ¿Adónde van madre e hija?
2. ¿Qué ve la hija?
3. ¿Qué quiere comprar ella?
4. Hay mucha gente allí?
5. ¿Adónde va una vez en casa?
6. ¿Dónde han puesto la fruta?
7. ¿Es moderna su casa?
8. ¿Cómo sabes?
9. ¿Qué abre ella?
10. ¿Qué saca de allí?
11. ¿Para qué lo necesita?
12. ¿Qué está haciendo?
13. ¿Qué puso en el plato?
14. ¿Qué usa para los ojos?
15. ¿Qué usa para la nariz?
16. ¿Qué más ha usado?

Picture Story 11

Perfect Picture Stories

English - 12

storm –
lightning –
strike –
roof –
fire –
burning –
firefighter –
ruins –

neighbors –
hammer –
wood –
paint –
build –
repair –
grateful –

1. What is the weather like today?
2. What happens to the tree?
3. Why are the birds leaving?
4. What happens to the roof?
5. What are the residents doing?
6. What is the house made of?
7. What do the firemen do?
8. What do they use?

9. How is the family feeling?
10. What do the neighbors decide?
11. What does the younger man say?
12. What does the older man say?
13. What does the woman say?
14. What do they help do?
15. Describe what they do.
16. How does the family feel now?

Español - 12

tempestad –
relámpago –
pega –
techo –
quemando –
bombero –
ruinas –

vecinos –
martillo –
madera –
pintar –
construir –
reparar –
agradecido –

1. ¿Qué tiempo hace hoy?
2. ¿Qué le pasa al árbol?
3. ¿Por qué se van los pájaros?
4. ¿Qué le pasa al techo y por qué?
5. ¿ Qué hacen los dueños?
6. ¿De qué está hecha la casa?
7. ¿Qué hacen los bomberos?
8. ¿Qué usan?

9. ¿Cómo se siente la familia?
10. ¿Qué deciden los vecinos?
11. ¿ Qué dice el hombre joven?
12. ¿ Qué dice el hombre mayor?
13. ¿Qué dice la señora?
14. ¿ Cómo les ayudan?
15. Describe lo qué hacen.
16. ¿Cómo se siente la familia?

Français 12

tempête
éclair
taper
toît
feu
brûler
pompier
ruines

voisin
marteau
bois
peinture
construire
réparer
reconnaissant

1. Quel temps fait-il aujourd'hui?
2. Qu'arrive-t-il à l'arbre?
3. Pourquoi est-ce-que les oiseaux S'en vont?
4. Qu'est-ce qui arrive au toît et pourquoi?
5. Que font les résidents et pourquoi?
6. De quoi est construite la maison?
7. Que font les pompiers?
8. Qu'est-ce qu'ils utilisent?

9. Comment se sent la famille?
10. Que décident les voisins?
11. Que dit l'homme plus jeune?
12. Que dit l'home plus â?
13. Que dit la femme?
14. Qu'est-ce qu'ils à faire?
15. Décrivez ce qu'ils font.
16. Comment se sent la famille maintenant?

Perfect Picture Stories for Language Learning © Lonnie Dai Zovi

Perfect Picture Stories

English - 13

Band –
guitar –
drums –
microphone –
singing –
play –
drumstick –
string -
break -
drop -
rain -
audience -
concert -
discouraged -
contract –
to sign –

1. Describe the members of the band.
2. What happens to the guitar player?
3. What happens to the drummer?
4. What happens to the singer?
5. How do they feel?
6. What does the guitarist do the next day?
7. What does the drummer do the next day?
8. What happens the next time they perform?
9. What does the audience do?
10. How is the band feeling now?
11. Where do they go?
12. Who comes to talk to them there?
13. What does he say to them?
14. What do they say to him?
15. How will their future be?

Français 13

groupe
guitare
batterie
microphone
chanter
jouer
baguette
ficelle
pause
goutte
pluie
public
concert
découragér
contrat
signer

1. Décrivez les membres du groupe.
2. Qu'arrive-t-il a guitariste?
3. Qu'arrive-t-il au batteur?
4. Qu'arrive-t-il au chanteur?
5. Comment se sentent-ils?
6. Que fait le guitariste le landemain?
7. Que fait le batteur le landemain?
8. Qu'arrive-t-il la prochaine fois qu'ils jouent?
9. Que fait le public?
10. Comment se sent le groupe maintenant?
11. Où vont-ils?
12. Qui vient leur parler?
13. Que leur dit-il?
14. Que leur disent-ils?
15. Comment va être leur futur?

Español - 13

banda –
guitarra –
bateria –
micrófono –
palillo –
cuerda –
romper -
dejar caer -
llover -
público -
concierto -
desanimado -
contracto -
firmar –

1. Describe la banda.
2. ¿Qué le pasa al guitarrista?
3. ¿Qué le pasa al baterista?
4. ¿Qué le pasa a la cantante?
5. ¿Cómo se sienten?
6. ¿Qué hace el guitarrista ahora?
7. ¿Qué hace el baterista ahora?
8. ¿Qué les pasa cuando tocan otra vez?
9. ¿Qué hace el público?
10. ¿Cómo se siente la banda?
11. ¿Adónde van después?
12. ¿Quién viene a hablarles?
13. ¿Qué les dice?
14. ¿Qué le contestan?
15. ¿Cómo será su futuro?

Picture Story 13

Perfect Picture Stories

English - 14

extraterrestrial –
king –
earth –
camera –
take pictures –
cactus –
desert –

1. Who is giving orders?
2. What is he saying?
3. Who are these beings?
4. Where are they going?
5. What is their purpose there?
6. What does the first one see?
7. What does he do there?
8. What does the second one see?

9. What does he do there?
10. What is he thinking?
11. What does the third one see?
12. What does he do and why?
13. Where is the fourth one?
14. What does he do?
15. What does he think?
16. What do they all tell the king?

Français 14

serpent
scorpion
appareil-photo
défilé
ferme
igloo
ours blanc

extra-terrestre
roi
terre
vaisseau spacial
fair des photos
cactus
désert

1. Qui donne des ordres?
2. Que dit-il?
3. Qui sont ces personnes?
4. Où vont-ils?
5. Quel est leur but ici?
6. Que voit le premier?
7. Que fait-il?
8. Que voit le deuxième?

9. Que fait-il ?
10. Que pense-t-il?
11. Que voit le troisième?
12. Que fait-il et pourquoi?
13. Où est le quatrième?
14. Que fait-il?
15. Que pense-t-il?
16. Que disent-ils tous au roi?

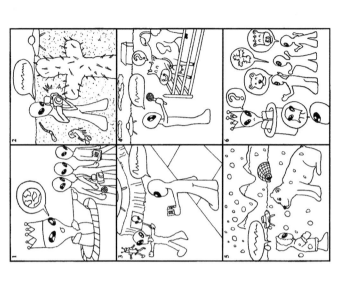

Español - 14

serpiente -
alacrán -
nave espacial -
desfile -
granja -
iglú -
oso polar -

extraterrestre –
rey –
tierra –
cámara –
sacar fotos –
cacto –
desierto -

1. ¿Quién da ordenes aquí?
2. ¿Qué les dice?
3. ¿Quiénes son ellos?
4. ¿Adónde van?
5. ¿Cuál es su propósito?
6. ¿Qué ve el primero?
7. ¿Qué hace allí?
8. ¿Qué ve el segundo?

9. ¿Qué hace él allí?
10. ¿Qué estará pensando?
11. ¿Qué ve el tercero?
12. ¿Qué hace y por qué?
13. ¿Dónde está el cuarto?
14. ¿Qué hace él?
15. ¿Qué está pensando?
16. ¿Qué le dicen al rey?

Picture Story 14

Perfect Picture Stories

English – 15

vacation –
cellular phone –
computer –
umbrella –
mermaid –
rocks -

tube -
starfish -
sea horse -
octopus -
braid -
believe -

1. Where is this family?
2. What are they doing there?
3. What types of people are they?
4. What is the father doing?
5. What is the mother doing?
6. What is the daughter doing?
7. What does she see?
8. What does she ask her mother?

9. Who does she talk to in the water?
10. Where does she go?
11. How does she breathe?
12. What does she ride on?
13. What does the octopus do?
14. What does she tell her parents?
15. What does her dad do?
16. What does her mom do?

Français 15

vacances
téléphone portable
ordinateur
parasol
sirène
rochers

tuyau
étoile de mer
hippocampe
pieuvre
tresse
croire

1. Où est la famille?
2. Que font-ils ici?
3. Quelle sorte de gens sont-ils?
4. Que fait le père?
5. Que fait la mère?
6. Que fait la fille?
7. Que voit-elle?
8. Que demande-t-elle à sa mère?

9. A qui parle-t-elle sous l'eau?
10. Où va-t-elle?
11. Comment respire-t-elle?
12. Sur quoi fait-elle un tour?
13. Que fait la pieuvre?
14. Que dit-elle à ses parents?
15. Que fait son père?
16. Que fait sa mère?

Español – 15

vacaciones -
celular -
computadora -
paraguas -
sirena -
piedras -

tubo -
estrella de mar -
caballo de mar -
pulpo -
trenza -
creer -

1. ¿Dónde está la familia?
2. ¿Qué están haciendo allí?
3. Descríbelos.
4. ¿Qué hace el papá?
5. ¿Qué hace la mamá?
6. ¿Qué hace la hija?
7. ¿Qué ve la niña?
8. ¿Qué le pregunta a su mamá?

9. ¿A quién le habla en el agua?
10. ¿Adónde va ?
11. ¿Cómo puede respirar?
12. ¿En qué se pasea?
13. ¿Qué hace el pulpo?
14. ¿Qué les dice a sus padres?
15. ¿Qué hace su mamá?
16. ¿Qué hace su papá?

Picture Story 15

Perfect Picture Stories

English- 16

homeless —
alley —
barefoot —
rags —
job —
want ads —
newspaper -

office building -
shake hands -
drowning -
save -
hero -
lifeguard -
opportunity -

1. Where is the man?
2. What is he doing?
3. What does he look like?
4. What does he find out?
5. Where does he go?
6. Why does he go there?
7. What happens when he arrives?

8. How does he feel?
9. Where does he go now?
10. What does he see?
11. What does he do?
12. What happens as a result?
13. Describe his looks now.
14. How will his life change?

Français 16

sans-abri
ruelle
pieds nus
chiffon
travail
petite annonce
journal

siege social
serrer la main
se noyer
sauver
héros
maître-nageur
opportunite

1. Où est l'homme?
2. Que fait-il?
3. De quoi a-t-il l'air?
4. Que lit-il?
5. Ou va-t-il?
6. Pourquoi va-t-il?

7. Qu'arrive-t-il quand il arrive?
8. Comment se sent-il?

9. Où va-t-il maintenant?
10. Que voit-il?
11. Que fait-il?
12. Qu'arrive-t-il au finalment?
13. Décrivez son apparence maintenant?
14. De quelle manière sa vie va-t-elle changer?
15. Quel est son nouveau travail?

Español - 16

desamparado —
callejón —
descalzo —
trapos —
trabajo —
anuncios —
periódico —

edificio de oficinas -
darse la mano -
ahogandose -
rescatar -
héroe -
salvavidas -
oportunidad —

1. ¿Dónde está el hombre?
2. ¿Qué está haciendo?
3. Describelo.
4. ¿De qué se entera?
5. ¿Adónde va inmediatamente?
6. ¿Por qué?
7. ¿Qué ve cuando llega?
8. ¿Cómo se siente?

9. ¿Adónde va ahora?
10. ¿Qué ve al caminar por la playa?
11. ¿Qué se le ocurre hacer?
12. ¿Tuvo éxito en sus esfuerzos?
13. ¿Qué pasó como resultado?
14. Describe al señor ahora.
15. ¿Cómo cambió su vida?

Picture Story 16

Perfect Picture Stories

English - 17

costume –
witch –
dark haired –
blonde –
party –
refreshments -

cat -
pumpkin -
monster -
mistake -
hold hand –
mask –

1. What is the woman doing?
2. What does the mother look like?
3. What does the daughter dress as?
4. What is the other mother doing?
5. What does she look like?
6. What does her daughter look like?
7. Where do they go?
8. How are the other people dressed?

9. What is everybody doing?
10. What do the mothers do?
11. What happens outside?
12. What do they realize?
13. How do they solve their problem?
14. How does everyone feel?
15. What have they learned?

Español - 17

disfraz –
bruja –
moreno –
rubio –
fiesta –
refrescos -

gato -
calabaza -
monstro -
error -
tomar la mano -
máscara –

1. ¿Qué hace la mujer?
2. Descríbela.
3. ¿De qué se disfraza la hija?
4. ¿Qué hace la otra mamá?
5. Descríbela.
6. Describa a la hija.
7. ¿Adónde van?

8. ¿Cómo están disfrazados los otros?
9. ¿Qué están haciendo todos allí?
10. ¿Qué hacen después de la fiesta?
11. ¿Qué pasa afuera?
12. ¿De qué se dan cuenta?
13. ¿Cómo resuelven el problema?
14. ¿Ahora cómo se sienten?

Français 17

costume
sorcière
cheveux noirs
blonde
fête
rafraichissements

chat
citrouille
monstre
faute
tenir la main
masque

1. Que fait la femme?
2. De quoi la mère ressemble-t-elle?
3. En quoi s'est deguisse la fille?
4. Que fait l'autre mère?
5. A quoi la ressemble-t-elle?

6. De quoi la fille ressemble-t-elle?
7. Où vont-elles?
8. Comment sont habillées les autres gens ?

9. Que font tout les gens?
10. Que font les mères après la fête?
11. Que se passe-t-il dehors?
12. De quoi se redent-ells compte?
13. Comment résoudent-elles le problème?
14. Comment se sent tout le monde?
15. Où vont-elles maintenant?

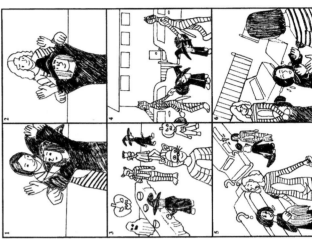

Perfect Picture Stories for Language Learning © Lonnie Dai Zovi

Picture Story 17

Perfect Picture Stories

English - 18

plans –
camping –
tent –
lake –
pack –
forest –
matches –
logs -

1. What is the family discussing?
2. What do the parents want to do?
3. What do the children want to do?
4. What has been decided?
5. What do they pack in the car?
6. Where do they go?
7. What happens to the children?
8. What happens to the plates?

wind -
blow -
bear -
chase -
bees -
motel -
swimming pool -
comfort –

9. What is the dad trying to do?
10. Why can't he do it?
11. What does the bear do?
12. Where do they hide from the bear?
13. What happens to the tent?
14. Where do they spend their vacation?
15. What do the children do?
16. What do the parents do?

Español – 18

planes –
acampando –
tienda –
lago –
empacar –
bosque –
fósforos –
leña -

1. ¿Qué planea la familia?
2. ¿Qué quieren los padres?
3. ¿Qué quieren los hijos?
4. ¿Qué deciden hacer por fin?
5. ¿Qué empacan en el carro?
6. ¿Adónde van?
7. ¿Qué les pasa a los niños?
8. ¿Qué pasa con los platos?

viento -
soplar -
oso -
perseguir -
abejas -
motel -
piscina -
comodidad –

9. ¿Qué trata de hacer papá?
10. ¿Por qué no puede hacerlo?
11. ¿Qué hace el oso?
12. ¿Adónde van a escaparse del oso?
13. ¿Qué pasa a la tienda?
14. ¿Dónde pasan sus vacaciones?
15. ¿Adónde van los niños?
16. ¿Qué hacen los padres?

Français 18

projets
camping
tente
lac
faire les bagages
forêt
allumettes
bûche

1. Que discute la famille?
2. Que veulent faire les parents?
3. Que veulent faire les enfants?
4. Qu'est-ce qu'on a décidé?
5. Qu'mettent-ils dans la voiture?
6. Où vont-ils?
7. Qu'est-ce qui arrive aux enfants?
vont-ils maintenant?
8. Qu'est-ce qui arrive aux assiettes?

vent
faire voler
ours
chasse
abeilles
môtel
piscine
confort

9. Qu'essaie de faire le père?
10. Pourquoi ne peut-il pas le faire?
11. Que fait l'ours?
12. Où vont-ils pour échapper à l'ours?
13. Qu'arrive-t-il a la tente?
14. Comment se sent tout le monde?
15. Où vont-ils maintenant ?

Picture Story 18

Perfect Picture Stories

English - 19

birthday –
initiation –
grandparents –
deaf –
cane –
overalls –
truck –

1. What does the woman look like?
2. What does her husband look like?
3. What have they received?
4. Do they seem happy about it?
5. Where are they going to go?
6. Why do they need to go there?
7. How do they get there?
8. About how long of a trip is it?

trip -
present -
toy store -
stuffed animals -
dolls -
choose -
identical –

9. What type of store do they enter?
10. What do they see there?
11. What do they decide to buy?
12. What do they see at the party?
13. How do they feel about that?
14. Who is the little girl?
15. What will she do with her gifts?

Français 19

anniversaire
invitation
grand-parents
sourd
canne
salopette
camion
ferme

voyage
cadeau
magasin de jouets
peluche
poupée
choisir
identique

1. De quoi a l'air la vieille dame?
2. De quoi a l'air son mari?
3. Qu'ont-ils reçu?
4. Ont-ils content de cela?
5. Où vont-ils aller?
6. Pourquoi ont-ils besoin d'y aller?
7. Comment sont-ils allés là-bas?
8. Plus ou moins combien de temps dure le voyage?
9. Dans quel genre de magasin entrent-ils?
10. Que voient-ils?
11. Que se décident-ils à acheter?
12. Que voient-ils à la fête?
13. Qu'en pensent-ils?
14. Qui est la petite fille?
15. Que va-t-elle faire avec ses cadeaux?
16. Devraient-ils échanger le cadeau?
Pourquoi?

Español - 19

cumpleaños –
invitación –
abuelos –
sordo –
bastón –
pecheras –
camión –
granja –

viaje -
regalo -
juguetería -
animales de peluche -
muñecas -
escoger -
idéntico -

1. Describe a la mujer.
2. Describe al hombre.
3. ¿Qué recivieron?
4. ¿Parecen contentos al recibirlo?
5. ¿Adónde van?
6. ¿Por qué?
7. ¿Cómo llegan allí?
8. ¿A qué tipo de tienda entran?
9. ¿Qué ven allí?
10. ¿Qué deciden comprar?
11. ¿Qué ven en la fiesta?
12. ¿Cómo les hace sentir?
13. ¿Quién es la niña?
14. ¿Qué hará con sus regalos?

Perfect Picture Stories

English - 20

bake –
groceries –
bags –
wrap –
freeze –
steaks –

suitcases –
snack –
defrost –
hungry –
rotten –
smelly –

1. What is the wife doing?
2. Where did the husband go?
3. What did he do there?
4. What do they do with the meat?
5. What do they do with the hot bread?
6. Where do they put them both?
7. Where are they going?

8. Where do they stay?
9. What does she do when she's hungry?
10. What happens when she opens the bread?
11. What are their reactions?
12. Why did this happen?
13. What will they do now?

Français 20

cuire
épiceries
sacs
emballer
congeler
steak

valise
casse-croûte
décongeler
affamé
pourri
sentant

1. Que fait la femme?
2. Où a été le mari?
3. Qu'y a-t-il fait?
4. Que font-ils avec la viande?
5. Que font-ils avec le pain frais?
6. Où les mettent-ils?
7. Qu'est-ce qu'ils ont l'intention de faire avec le pain
8. Où vont-ils?

9. Où restent-ils?
10. Que fait-elle quand elle a faim?
11. Qu'est-ce que se passe quand elle ouvre le pain?
12. Quelles réagissent-ils?
13. Pourquoi est-ce que cela arrive?
14. Que vont-ils faire maintenant?
15. Devront-ils congeler le pain la prochaine fois?

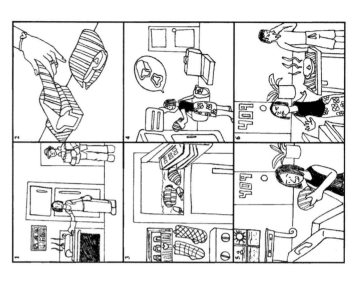

Español - 20

hornear –
comestibles –
bolsas –
envolver –
congelar –
bistecs –

maletas –
bocado –
descongelar –
hambre–
podrido –
apestoso –

1. ¿Qué esta 'haciendo la esposa?
2. ¿De dónde vino el esposo?
3. ¿Por qué?
4. ¿Qué hacen con la carne?
5. ¿Qué hacen con el pan fresco?
6. ¿Dónde lo ponen?
7. ¿Qué planean hacer con el pan?

8. ¿Adónde van?
9. ¿Qué hace cuando tiene hambre?
10. ¿Qué pasa cuando abre el "pan"?
11. ¿Cuál es su reacción?
12. ¿Cómo lo pasó?
13. Ahora ¿qué harán?

Perfect Picture Stories

English - 21

worker –
to clean –
to shine –
glass –
walk into –
to mop –

floor –
wax –
to slip –
to fall –
to dust –
to complain –

1. Where is the man right now?
2. What is he doing?
3. Why is he doing it?
4. What does the older man do?
5. Why does he do that?
6. Is he seriously hurt?
7. What is the worker's second job?
8. Who helps him?

9 What happens to the woman?
10. How and why did she fall?
11. What is the worker's third job?
12. What doesn't he notice?
13. How does the man react?
14. What is the result of all this?
15. Is it fair?
16. Why or why not?

Français 21

ouvrier
nettoyer
briller
vitre
rentrer dans
balayer

plancher
cire
glisser
tomber
épousseter
se plaindre

1. Où est l'homme en ce moment?
2. Que fait-il?
3. Pourquoi le fait-il?
4. Que fait l'homme plus â   ge?
5. Pourquoi fait-il cela?
6. Est-il serieusement blessé?
7. Quel est le deuxieme travail de l'ouvrier?
8. Qui l'aide?

9. Qu'est-ce qui arrive-t-il à la femme?
10. Comment et pourquoi tombe-t-elle?
11. Quel est le troisième travail de l'ouvrier?
12. Que ne remarque-t-il pas?
13. Comment réagit l'homme?
14. Quel est le résultat de tout cela?
15. C'est juste ça?
16. Pourquoi?

Español - 21

empleado –
limpiar –
brillar –
vidrio –
chocarse –
trapear –

piso –
cera –
resbalarse –
caerse –
quitar el polvo –
quejarse –

1. ¿Dónde está el hombre ahora?
2. ¿Qué está haciendo?
3. ¿Por qué?
4. ¿Qué hace el otro hombre?
5. ¿Por qué?
6. ¿Está seriamente lastimado?
7. ¿Cuál es su segunda tarea?
8. ¿Quién le ayuda?

9. ¿Qué le pasa a la mujer?
10. ¿Cómo y por qué se cayó?
11. ¿Cuál es su tercera tarea?
12. ¿De qué no fija?
13. ¿Cómo se reaciona el hombre?
14. ¿Cuál es el resultado de todo esto?
15. ¿Es justo? ¿Por qué?

Picture Story 21

Perfect Picture Stories

English – 22

poverty –
bills –
unemployed –
desperate –
apply –
job –

1. Who is in the room?
2. What are they talking about?
3. What does their house look like?
4. How do they feel right now?
5. What does the boy want to do?
6. Where does he go first?
7. What does he say?
8. What does the man answer?

bakery -
drugstore -
hardware store -
discouraged -
pizzeria -
deliver –

9. Where does he go second?
10. Does he have luck there?
11. Where is his third stop?
12. Is he successful there?
13. Where does he g o last?
14. What does the owner say?
15. What is his new job?
16. How will things change for him?

Español - 22

pobreza —
cuentas —
desempleado —
desesperado —
hacer solicitud —
trabajo -

1. ¿Quién está en el cuarto?
2. ¿De qué están hablando?
3. ¿Cómo es su casa?
4. ¿Cómo se sienten ahora?
5. ¿Qué quiere hacer el joven?
6. ¿Adónde va primero?
7. ¿Qué le pregunta?
8. ¿Qué contesta el hombre?

panadería -
farmacia -
ferretería -
desanimado -
pizzería -
entregar –

9. ¿Adónde va después?
10. ¿Tiene suerte allí?
11. ¿Cuál es su tercera parada?
12. ¿Tiene éxito allí?
13. ¿Adónde va ultimamente?
14. ¿Qué le dice el dueño?
15. ¿Cuál es su nuevo trabajo?
16. ¿Cómo cambiaría su vida?

Français 22

pauvreté
facture
sans-emploi
désespéré
appliquer
travail

1. Qui est dans la pièce?
2. De quoi parlent-ils?
3. Comment est leur maison?
4. Comment se sentent-ils en ce moment?
5. Que veut faire le garçon?
6. Où va-t-il en premier?
7. Que dit-il?
8. Que réponds l'homme?

boulangerie
drugstore
quincaillerie
découragé
pizzeria
livrer

9. Où va-t-il en deuxième fois?
10. A-t-il de bonne chance cette fois?
11. Où est son troisième arrêt?
12. A-t-il de la chance ici?
13. Où va-t-il enfin?
14. Que dit le propriétaire?
15. Quel est son nouveau travail?
16. Comment la vie va-t-elle changer pour lui ?

Picture Story 22

Perfect Picture Stories

English – 23

princess —
knight —
queen —
dreams —
castle —
marriage —
king —

throne -
to object -
tower -
escape -
frog -
pond -
convert -

1. Who is sitting on the bricks?
2. What are they talking about?
3. What does the princess want?
4. What will she get instead?
5. Does her mother seem to care?
6. Who comes to visit her father?
7. What does the older man want?
8. What does the king say?

9. Where does the princess sleep?
10. What does she attempt?
11. Where does she run?
12. What kind of night is it?
13. What does she do at the pond?
14. Why does she do that?
15. What has happened to her?
16. What do her parents think?

Español - 23

princesa -
caballero —
reina —
sueños -
castillo —
casamiento —
rey —

trono -
protestar -
torre -
escaparse -
rana -
río -
convertirse —

1. ¿Quién se sienta en los ladrillos?
2. ¿De qué hablan?
3. ¿Qué quiere la princesa?
4. ¿Qué tendrá en su lugar?
5. ¿Le importa a la madre?
6. ¿Quién visita al rey?
7. ¿Qué quiere el viejo?
8. ¿Qué le dice el rey?

9. ¿Dónde duerme la princesa?
10. ¿Qué trata de hacer?
11. ¿Adónde corre?
12. ¿Cómo está la noche?
13. ¿Qué hace en el estanque?
14. ¿Por qué?
15. ¿Qué le ha pasado?
16. ¿Qué piensan sus padres?

Français 23

princesse
chevalier
reine
rêve
château
mariage
roi

trône
sésapprouver
tour
échapper
grenouille
fleuve
convertir

1. Qui est assis sur les briques?
2. De quoi parlent-ils?
3. Que veut la princesse?
4. Que va-t-elle recevoir à la place?
5. Est-ce-que sa mère a l'air de s'en préoccuper?
6. Qui vient visiter son père?
7. Que veut le viel homme?
8. Que dit le roi ?

9. Où dort la princesse?
10. Qu'essaie-t-elle de faire?
11. Où court-elle?
12. Quel sorte de nuit est-ce?
13. Que fait-elle sur l'eétain?
14. Pourquoi fait-elle cela?
15. Que lui est-il arrive?
16. Que pensent ses parents?

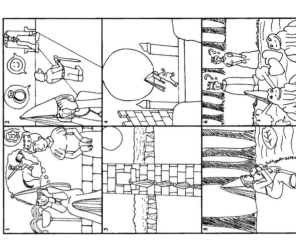

Picture Story 23

Perfect Picture Stories

English - 24

braid –
shopping –
weekly –
shopping cart –
shampoo –
cereal -

milk carton -
detergent -
full -
groceries -
cashier -
hidden —

1. Where does the father put his girl?
2. Where are they?
3. What do they need to do?
4. What do they put in the basket first?
5. Do they eat healthily?
6. What do they buy next?
7. How does the daughter help?
8. Is the dad paying attention?
9. What happened to his daughter?
10. What is he thinking?
11. Does he call her name?
12. Where has his daughter been?
13. What is everyone's reaction?

Français 24

tresser
shopping
hebdomadaire
charrette
shampoing
céréales

boîte lait
détersif
plein
épiceries
caissier
caisse

1. Où le père mets-il sa fille?
2. Où sont-ils?
3. Qu'ont-ils besoin de faire?
4. Que mettent-ils dans le charrette premièrement?
5. Mangent-ils de la nourriture saine?
6. Qu'achètent-ils ensuite?
7. De quelle manière la fille aide-t-elle son père?
8. Est-ce-que le père fait attention?
9. Qu'est-il arrive à sa fille?
10. Que pense-t-il?
11. Où était sa fille?
12. Quelle est la réaction de tous?
13. Nommez quelques choses qu'ils ont acheté?

Español - 24

trenza –
ir de compras –
semanal –
carrito –
champú –
cereal -

leche -
detergente -
lleno -
comestibles -
cajero -
escondido -

1. ¿Dónde le ha puesto a la hija?
2. ¿Dónde están ?
3. ¿Qué necesitan hacer?
4. ¿Qué escogen primero?
5. ¿Cómen comida sana?
6. ¿Qué compran después?
7. ¿Cómo ayuda la hija al padre?
8. ¿Presta atención el padre?
9. ¿Qué le ha pasado a la hija?
10. ¿Qué está pensando?
11. ¿Dónde habiá estado?
12. ¿Cómo reaccionan todos

Perfect Picture Stories

English - 25

bored –
relaxing –
couch –
living room –
yard –
leaves -

1. Where are the children?
2. What are they doing?
3. What month might it be?
4. Why do you think that?
5. What does the father look at?
6. What does he want them to do?
7. What does he give them?
8. What does he do as they work?

9. Are the children having fun?
10. What do they plan to do?
11. What does the boy do?
12. What do they do later?
13. What will the father say?

Español - 25

aburrido –
relajar –
sofá –
sala –
yarda (patio) –
hojas –

columpio –
resbaladero –
rastrillos –
rastrillar –
bolsa –
montón –

1. ¿Dónde están los niños?
2. ¿Qué están haciendo?
3. ¿Qué estación del año será?
4. ¿Por qué piensas así?
5. ¿Qué ve el padre?
6. ¿Qué quiere que haga?

7. ¿Qué les da el padre?
8. ¿Qué hace mientra trabajan?
9. ¿Se divierten los niños?
10. ¿Qué planean hacer?
11. ¿Qué hace el niño?
12. ¿Qué hacen después?
13. ¿Qué les dirá el padre?

Français 25

ennuyé
délassant
canapé
salon
cour
feuille

balaçoire
glisser
râteau
ratisser
sac
tas

1. Où sont les enfants?
2. Que font-ils?
   faire?
3. Quel mois peut-il être?
4. Pourquoi pensez-vous cela?
5. Que regarde le père?
6. Que veut-il qu'ils fassent?
7. Que leur donne-t-il?
8. Que fait-il pendant qu'ils travaillent?

9. Est-ce-que les enfants s'amusent?
10. De quoi ont-ils l'intention de
11. Que fait le garçon?
12. Que font-ils plus tard?
13. Que va dire le père?

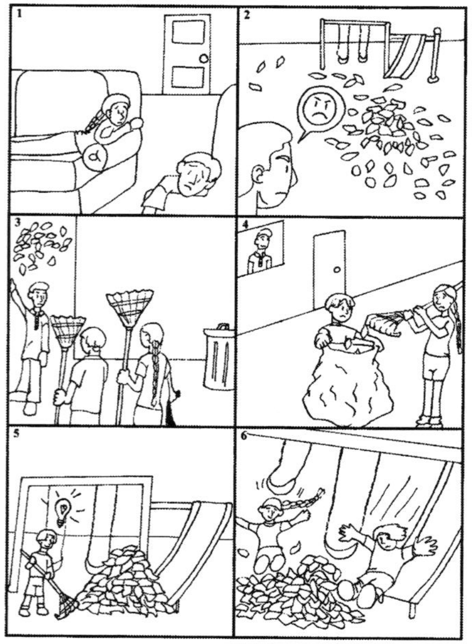

Perfect Picture Stories

English - 26

moving –
truck –
boxes –
carry –
stove –
refrigerator –
bags -

pillows -
kitchen -
bedroom -
toys -
bed -
towels -
asleep –

1. What is the family doing?
2. What is the boy holding?
3. Where is he taking it?
4. Why are they moving?
5. Who is helping them?
6. Who carries the refrigerator?
7. How many men carry the stove?
8. What does the boy help carry?
9. What has been moved to the bedroom?
10. What does the boy carry?
11. Is he helping a lot?
12. What does the mother carry in?
13. What does the father ask?
14. Where do they find their son?
15. What is he doing?

Français 26

déménager –
camion –
boîte -
porter –
cuisinière –
réfrigérateur –
sac -

oreiller
cuisine
chambre à coucher
jouet
lit
serviette
endormi

1. Que fait la famille?
2. Que tient le garçon?
3. Où l'emmène-t-il?
4. Pourquoi bougent-ils?
5. Qui les aide?
6. Qui porte le réfrigérateur?
7. Combien de personnes portent la cuisinière?
8. Qu'est-ce-que le garçon aide à porter?
9. Qu'est-ce qui a été déplacé dans la chambre?
10. Que porte le garçon?
11. Aide-t-il beaucoup?
12. Que porte la mère?
13. Que demande le père?
14. Est-il inquiet?
15. Où trouvent-ils leur fils?
16. Que fait-il?

Español - 26

mudarse –
camión –
cajas -
cargar –
estufa –
refrigerador –
bolsas -

almohadas –
cocina -
recámara -
juguetes-
cama -
toallas -
dormido –

1. ¿Qué hace la familia?
2. ¿Qué carga el niño?
3. ¿Adónde lo lleva?
4. ¿Por qué cambian casas?
5. ¿Quién les ayuda?
6. ¿Cuántos cargan el refrigerador?
7. ¿Cuántos cargan la estufa?
8. ¿Cómo ayuda el niño?
9. ¿Qué hay en la recámara?
10. ¿Qué carga el niño ahora?
11. ¿Ayuda mucho?
12. ¿Qué carga la madre?
13. ¿Qué pregunta el padre?
14. ¿Dónde encuentran al hijo?
15. ¿Qué está haciendo?

Picture Story 26

Perfect Picture Stories

English - 27

clowns –
balloons –
park –
dollar bill –
kite –
go up –

1. How many clowns are there?
2. What is in their hands?
3. What are they doing with them?
4. Where are the clowns?
5. What's the weather like?
6. How do you know?
7. What does the boy do?
8. Does anyone notice?

9. What does the short clown do?
10. What does he ask the other clown?
11. What happens to him?
12. Where does he go?
13. How does he get down?
14. What does the other clown say?
15. What does he answer?

Español - 27

payasos -
globos –
parque –
billete -
cometa –
subir -

rama -
lago -
barco -
tronco-
reventar -
deber-

1. ¿Cuántos payasos hay?
2. ¿Qué hay en sus manos?
3. ¿Qué hacen con ellos?
4. ¿Dónde están?
5. ¿Hace viento hoy?
6. ¿Cómo lo sabes?
7. ¿Qué hace un niño?
8. ¿Alguién se da cuenta?

9. ¿Qué hace el payaso más bajo?
10. ¿Qué le pide al otro payaso?
11. ¿Qué le pasa?
12. ¿Adónde va?
13. ¿Qué le pasa entonces?
14. ¿Qué le dice un payaso al otro?
15. ¿Qué le contesta?

branch -
lake -
boat -
tree trunk -
to pop -
to owe –

Français 27

clowns
ballons
parc
billet
cerf-volant
monter

branche
lac
bateau
tronc d'arbre
faire éclater
devoir

1. Combien de clowns y a-t-il?
2. Que tiennent-ils dans leurs mains?

3. Que font-ils avec ces choses?
4. Où sont-ils?
5. Fait-il du vent aujourd'hui?
6. Comment le savez-vous?
7. Que fait un jeune garçon?
8. Est-ce-que quelqu'un le remarque?

9. Que fait le plus petit clown?
10. Que demande-t-il du deuxième clown?
11. Que lui arrive-t-il?
12. Où va-t-il?
13. Comment descend-il?
14. Que lui dit le plus petit clown?
15. Que répond-t-il?

Picture Story 27

Perfect Picture Stories

English - 28

storm –
ship –
sink –
boat –
escape –
island –
sail –
palm trees –

1. What's the weather like?
2. What does the lightning do?
3. What happened to the ship?
4. What does the man do?
5. Why doesn't he use the motor?
6. What does he use instead?
7. What does he see in the distance?
8. What does the island look like?

camp fire –
tent –
coconuts –
monkey –
throw –
shelter –
civilization –
unknown –

9. What does he eat his first night?
10. Describe his first shelter.
11. Describe his second shelter.
12. How does he get coconuts?
13. Has he been there long?
14. What's the evidence?
15. What's on the side?
16. Will he ever find that out?

Español - 28

tempestad –
nave –
hundirse –
barco -
escaparse –
isla –
vela –
palmeras -

1. ¿Qué tiempo hace hoy?
2. ¿Qué hace el relámpago?
3. ¿Qué le pasa a la nave?
4. ¿Qué hace el hombre?
5. ¿Por qué no usa el motor?
6. ¿Qué usa en su lugar?
7. ¿Qué ve a la distancia?

fogata –
tienda -
cocos –
chango -
tirar -
refugio –
civilización -
desconocido-

9. ¿Qué come su primera noche?
10. Describe su primer refugio.
11. ¿Cómo es su segundo refugio?
12. ¿Cómo consigue cocos?
13. ¿Ha estado allí mucho tiempo?
14. ¿Cómo lo sabes?
15. ¿Qué hay en el otro lado de la isla?

Français 28

tempête
vaisseau
couler
bateau
échapper
île
naviguer
palmier

1.Quel temps fait-il aujourd'hui?
2.Que fait l'éclair?
3.Qu'arrive-t-il au bateau?
4.Que fait l'homme?
5.Pourquoi n'utilise-t-il pas le moteur?
6.Qu'utilise-t-il à la place?
7.Que voit-il au loin?
8.Comment est l'île?

feu de camp
tente
noix de coco
singe
jeter
abri
civilisation
inconnu

9.Que mange-t-il la première nuit?
10.Décrivez le premier abri.
11.Décrivez le deuxième abri.
12.Comment obtient-il des noix de coco?
13.A-t-il été ici depuis un longtemps?
14.Quelle en est l'evidence?
15.Qu'est-ce qu'il y a à l'autre côte?
16.Va-t-il un jour le découvrir?

Picture Story 28

Perfect Picture Stories

English - 29

dragon –
witch –
pet –
set store –
marshmallows –
hot dogs –

1. Describe the children.
2. How many are there?
3. What do they ask their mother?
4. Where does she take them?
5. What do they buy?
6. Describe their house.
7. What do the children cook?
8. How does the dragon help?

ride -
late -
fly -
fireplaces -
to warm –
to heat –

9. What happens if they miss the bus?
10. How does he help in the winter?
11. Where do they sleep in the winter?
12. How do they feel about their him?
13. How else might he help them?
14. Should they get a different pet?
15. Can the dragon be dangerous?

Español - 29

dragón –
bruja –
mascota –
tienda de mascotas –
bonbones –
salchichas –

paseo –
tarde –
volar –
chimenea –
calentar –

1. Describe a los niños.
2. ¿Cuántos niños hay?
3. ¿Quñe le piden a su mamá?
4. ¿Adoñnde las lleva?
5. ¿Qué compran?
6. Describe la casa.
7. ¿Qué preparan para la cena?
ayudar?

8. ¿Cómo les ayuda el dragón?
9. ¿Qué pasa si pierden el autobús?
10. ¿Cómo les ayuda en el invierno?
11. ¿Dónde duermen en el invierno?
12. ¿Cómo se siente de su dragón?
13. ¿En cuáles otras maneras les

Français 29

dragon
sorcière
animal familier
magasin d'animaux familiers
guimauves
saucissons

voyage
tard
voler
cheminée
réchauffer
chauffer

1. Décrivez les enfants?
2. Combien sont-ils?
3. Que demandent-ils à leur mère?
4. Où les emmène-t-elle?
5. Qu'achètent-ils?

6. Dans quelle sorte de maison vivent-ils?
7. Que préparent les enfants?
8. De quelle maniere est-ce-que le dragon aide?

9. Qu'arrive-t-il s'ils ratent le bus scolaire?
10. Comment aide-t-il pendant l'hiver?
11. Où dorment-ils pendant l'hiver?
12. Que pense-t-ils du dragon?
13. De quelle autre manière pourrait-il les aider?
14. Devraient-ils acheter un animal diffent?
15. Le dragon peut-il etre dangereux?

Picture Story 29

Perfect Picture Stories

English - 30

brace -
accident -
stretcher -
ambulance -
crash -
crippled -
cast -
soccer -
jealous -
determination -
improve -
cobwebs -
race -
run -
win -
trophy -

1. What happened to the cars?
2. How many are there?
3. How's the passenger?
4. Where is he now?
5. What happened to his leg?
6. What did the doctor say?
7. What are his parents doing?
8. What happens in the park?
9. What's the boy doing?
10. What does his leg look like?
11. What has happened gradually?
12. What is the doctor's reaction?
13. Who enters a race?
14. How does he do in the race?
15. How do his parents feel?
16. How is his leg now?

Español - 30

accidente -
camilla -
ambulancia -
choque -
cojo -
yeso -
fútbol -
celoso -
aparato ortopédico -
determinación -
mejorarse -
telarañas -
carrera -
correr -
ganar -
trofeo -

1. ¿Qué les pasó a los dos carros?
2. ¿Cómo pasó?
3. ¿Qué le pasó al pasajero?
4. ¿Dónde está ahora?
5. ¿Qué le pasó a su pierna?
6. ¿Qué dijo el doctor?
7. ¿Qué hacen sus padres?
8. ¿Qué pasa en el parque?
9. ¿Qué hace el niño?
10. ¿Cómo está su pierna?
11. ¿Qué pasa después de un tiempo?
12. ¿Cuál es la reacción del doctor?
13. ¿Quién está en la carrera?
14. ¿Cuál es el resultado?
15. ¿Cómo se sienten los padres?
16. ¿Ahora cómo queda su pierna?

Français 30

accident
brancard
ambulance
accident de voiture
estropié
plâtre
football
jaloux
attelle
détermination
améliorer
toile d'araignée
course
courir
gagner
trophée

1. Qu'est-il arrive aux deux voitures?
2. Que s'est-il passé?
3. Qu'est-ce qui est-il arrivé au passager?
4. Où est-il maintenant?
5. Qu'est-ce qui est arrive à sa jambe?
6. Qu'a dit le médecin?
7. Que font ses parents?
8. Qu'arrive-t-il au parc?
9. Que fait le garçon?
10. Comment paraî sa jambe?
11. Qu'est-il arrivé après un moment?
12. Quelle est la réaction du docteur?
13. Qui participe à la course?
14. Comment fait-il?
15. Comment se sentent les parents?
16. Comment va sa jambe maintenant?

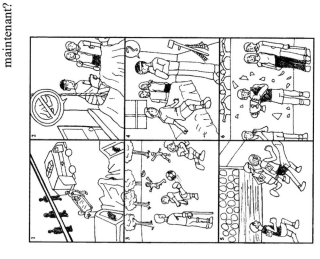

Picture Story 30

Perfect Picture Stories

English - 31

library –
steps –
park bench –
fantasy –
fairies –
shopping –

in love –
run into –
married –
disuse –
children –
pastime –

1. Who is on the stairs?
2. Is the girl coming or going?
3. What is this place?
4. What statues are in front?
5. What are they all carrying?
6. What's the mother doing?
7. What room are they in?
8. What is in the girl's room?
9. What is the girl holding?
10. What do the girls do in the park?
11. What are they reading about?
12. What are the other people doing?
13. What does she do as others shop?
14. What is her favorite pastime?
15. Who does she meet in the park?
16. Describe their future life.

Français 31

bibliothèque
marche
banc public
fantasie
fée
shopping

amoureux
rencontrer
marie
a l'abandon
enfants
passe-temps

1. Combien de gens y a-t-il dans l'escalier?
2. Est-ce-que la fille va ou revient?
3. Quel est cet endroit?
4. Quelles statues sont devant?
5. Que portent-ils tous?
6. Que fait la mère?
7. Dans quel piece sont-ils?
8. Qu'est-ce qu'il y a dans sa chambre?
9. Que tient la fille?
10. Que font les filles dans le parc?
11. De quel sujet est leur lecture?
12. Que font les autres personnes?
13. Que fait-elle pendant que les autres font dans du shopping?
14. Quel est son passe-temps favori ?
15. Qui rencontre-t-elle dans le parc?
16. Décrivez leur vie après leur rencontre.

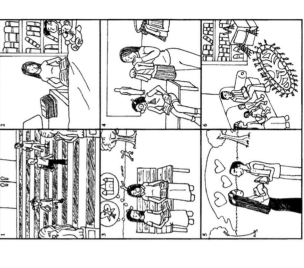

Español - 31

biblioteca –
escalones –
banca del parque –
fantasía –
hadas –
ir de compras –

enamorado –
encontrarse con –
casado –
fuera de operación –
hijos –
pasatiempos –

1. ¿Qué hay en los escalones?
2. ¿Viene o se va la joven?
3. ¿Qué es este lugar?
4. ¿Cuáles estatuas están enfrente?
5. ¿Qué están cargando todos?
6. ¿Qué hace la mamá?
7. Describe su cuarto.
8. ¿Qué lleva la niña?
9. ¿Qué hacen las niñas en el parque?
10. ¿De qué están leyendo?
11. ¿Qué hacen los otros?
12. ¿Qué hace ella mientras compran?
13. ¿A quién encuentra en el parque?
14. Describe su vida juntos.

Perfect Picture Stories

English - 32

neighborhood –
alternative –
garbage –
theater –
gentleman –
lady -

stuck -
push -
muddy -
sweaty -
exhausted -
grateful –

1. Where are the teen-agers?
2. What are they doing?
3. How are they dressed?
4. What is their hair like?
5. Do they appear kind?
6. Describe the neighborhood.
7. Who goes into the theater?
8. Do they like the teens?

9. What happens to the man's car?
10. What is the man doing?
11. Is he successful at it?
12. Who else is nearby?
13. Is anybody available to help?
14. What do the teen-agers do?
15. What does the gentleman do?
16. What is he thinking?

Français 32

voisinage
alternative
poubelle
théâtre
gentlilhomme
dame

coincé
pousser
boueux
moite
éxtenué
reconnaissant

1.Où se trouvent les jeunes gens?

2.Que font-ils?
3.Comment sont-ils habillés?
4.Comment sont leurs cheveux?
5.Quel genre de personnes peuvent-ils être?

6.Quel type de voisinage est-ce?
7.Qui va au théâtre?
8.De quelle façon regardent-ils les jeunes gens?

9.Qu'est-ce qui arrive à la voiture de l'homme?
10.Que fait l'homme?
11.Y réussit-il?
12.Qui d'autre est a proche?
13.Y a-t-il quelqu'un disponible pour les aider?
14.Que font les jeunes gens?
15.Que fait le gentilhomme?
16.Que pense-t-il?

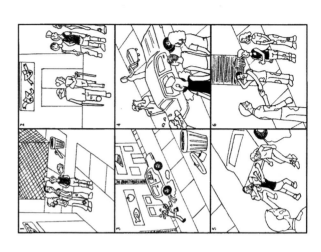

Español - 32

vecindario –
alternativo –
basura –
teatro –
caballero –
dama -

atascado -
empujar -
lodoso -
sudar –
exhausto -
agradecido –

1. ¿Dónde se reúnen los los jovenes?
2. ¿Qué hacen allí?
3. ¿Cómo están vestidos?
4. Describe sus peinados.
5. ¿Qué tipo de personas serán?
6. ¿Qué tipo de vecindario es?
7. ¿Quién entra al teatro?
8. ¿Cómo mira él a los jovenes?

9. ¿Qué pasa con aquel coche?
10. ¿Qué hace el hombre?
11. ¿Tiene éxito?
12. ¿Quién más está cerca?
13. ¿Hay alguién que ayude?
14. ¿Qué hacen los jovenes?
15. ¿Qué hace el caballero?
16. ¿Qué está pensando?

Picture Story 32

Perfect Picture Stories

English – 33

playing –
pile –
toys –
stuffed animals –
movement –
mysterious -

unexplained -
ghost -
haunted -
mouse -
scared -
mouse trap –
wind up –

1. What is the boy doing?
2. Describe his toys.
3. What does he look at?
4. What's the toy pile doing?
5. Where does he go?
6. What does he tell his mom?
7. Does she believe him?
8. What does she do?
9. How does she explain it?
10. What does she get?
11. What does she plan to do?
12. What happens when she moves the toys?
13. What do they see?
14. How do they react?

Español - 33

jugando –
montón –
juguetes –
animales de peluche –
movimiento –
misterioso –
inexplicable –

fantasma -
embrujado -
ratón -
asustado -
trampa para ratones -
darle cuerda -

1. ¿ Qué hace el niño?
2. Describe sus juguetes.
3. ¿Qué está mirando?
4. ¿Qué hace el montón de juguetes?
5. ¿A dónde va a él?
6. ¿Qué le dice a su madre?
7. ¿Le cree su madre?
8. ¿Qué hace ella?
9. ¿Qué piensa que es la causa?
10. ¿Qué va a conseguir?
11. ¿Qué va a hacer con ella?
12. ¿Qué pasa cuando remueve el montón de juguetes?
13. ¿Qué hace el juguete?

Français 33

jouant
tas
jouet
peluches
remonter
mouvement
mystérieux

inexplicable
fantôme
hanté
piège à souris
souris
peureux
conclure

1. Que fait le petit garçon?
2. Qu'est-ce qu'il y a comme jouets?
3. Que regarde-t-il?
4. Que fait le tas de jouets?
5. Où va-t-il?
6. Que dit-il à sa mère?
7. Le croit-elle?
8. Que fait-elle?
9. Que pense-t-elle être à l'origine de cela?
10. Que va-t-elle chercher?
11. Qu'a-t-elle l'intention de faire avec cela?
12. Que se passe-t-il quand elle bouge les jouets?
13. Que fait le jouet?

Perfect Picture Stories

English - 34

stereo –
rock star –
singer –
famous –
infatuated –
pay attention –

1. Where is the girl?
2. What is she doing?
3. Describe her room.
4. Who runs through the park?
5. What are they fans doing?
6. Why are they doing that?
7. Where is he going?
8. What is the girl doing in class?

9. What should she be doing?
10. Who knocks on the door?
11. What does he give the singer?
12. What does the singer do?
13. How does the girl react?
14. What do the two do next?
15. What will their life be like?

Español - 34

estereo –
estrella de rock –
cantante –
famoso –
enamorarse –
prestar atención –

1. ¿Dónde está la joven?
2. ¿Qué está haciendo?
3. Describe su cuarto.
4. ¿Quién corre por el parque?
5. ¿Qué hacen los chicos?
6. ¿Por qué?
7. ¿Adónde va él?
8. ¿Qué hace la joven en clase?

carta de amor –
solitario –
llamar por teléfono –
invitar –
encontrarse –
autógrafo –

9. ¿Qué debe hacer?
10. ¿Quién llama a la puerta?
11. ¿Qué le da al cantante?
12. ¿Qué hace él después?
13. ¿Cómo reacciona la chica?
14. ¿Qué hacen ellos después?
15. ¿Cómo será su vida ahora?

Français 34

stéréo
rock star
chanteur
bien connu
infatué
faire attention

lettre d'amour
se sentir seul
téléphoner à
inviter
autographe
rencontrer

1. Où est la jeune fille?
2. Que fait-elle?
3. Comment est sa chambre?
4. Qui traverse le parc en courant?
5. Que font les enfants?
6. Pourquoi font-ils cela?
7. Où va-t-il?
8. Que fait la fille en classe?

9. Que devrait-elle faire?
10. Qui frappe à la porte?
11. Que donne-t-il au chanteur?
12. Que fait le chanteur après?
13. Comment est-ce-que la fille réagit?
14. Que font les deux ensuite?
15. Comment va êztre leur vie?

Picture Story 34

Perfect Picture Stories

English - 35

cafeteria –
worker –
telephone number –
customer –
job –
uniform –

1. Where is the girl working?
2. Who else is there?
3. What are they doing?
4. Describe the young man.
5. What does he ask her?
6. What does she answer?

janitor -
closing time -
shift -
movies -
marriage proposal -
in love –

7. What does she notice one day?
8. Was it a coincidence?
9. What do they do after work?
10. Where do they go one evening?
11. What has happened over time?
12. What does the man do one day?

Español - 35

cafetería –
empleado -
número de teléfono –
cliente –
trabajo –
uniforme –

1. ¿Dónde trabaja la chica?
2. ¿Quién más está allá?
3. ¿Qué están haciendo?
4. ¿Qué le pregunta el chico?
5. ¿Qué le contesta?
6. Describe al chico.

conserje -
hora de cerrar -
turno -
cine -
casarse -
enamorado –

7. ¿De qué se da cuenta un día?
8. ¿Lo hizo a propósito?
9. ¿Qué hacen después del trabajo?
10. ¿Adónde van por la noche?
11. ¿Qué ha empezado a pasar?
12. ¿Qué hizo el joven un día?

Français 35

cafétéria
employé
numéro de téléphone
client
travail
uniforme

1. Où travaille la fille?
2. Qui d'autre est présent?
3. Que font-ils?
4. Que demande le jeune homme à la jeune fille?
5. De quoi a-t-il l'air?
6. Que répond-elle?

nettoyeur
heure de fermeture
changement
cinéma
demande en mariage
être amoureux

7. Que remarque-t-elle un jour?
8. Est-ce que c'est fait exprès?
9. Que font-ils après le travail?
10. Où vont-ils un soir?
11. Qu'est-ce qui arrive ensuite?
12. Que fait l'homme un jour?

Perfect Picture Stories

English - 36

bread –
cookies –
bake –
ingredients –
butter –
bowl –
measuring cup –

1. What are the children playing?
2. Are they hungry or bored?
3. What do they put on the table?
4. Are they forgetting anything?
5. What do they get from the cabinet?
6. What else is in the cabinet?
7. What does the boy do?

flour -
sugar -
salt -
eggs -
oven -
tray -
salty -

8. What does the girl do?
9. Where do they put the cookies?
10. What do the children do?
11. How do they taste?
12. What caused the bad taste?
13. What will they do with the cookies?

Français 36

ennuyé
biscuit
cuire
ingrédients
beurre
saladier
pichet gradué

1. Que décident de faire les enfants?
2. Ont-ils faim, ou s'ennuient-ils?
3. Que mettent-ils sur la table?
4. Ont-ils oublié quelque chose?
5. Que cherchent-ils dans le placard?
6. Quoi d'autre se trouve dans le placard?
7. Que fait le garçon?

farine
sucre
sel
oeufs
four
plateau
salé

8. Que fait la fille?
9. Où mettent-ils les biscuits?
10. Que font les enfants?
11. Comment est le goût?
12. Que s'est-il passé?
13. Comment peuvent-ils améliorer les biscuits ?

Español - 36

aburrido -
galletas -
hornear -
ingredientes –
mantequilla –
taza de medir -

1. ¿Qué planean los niños?
2. ¿Tienen hambre?
3. ¿Qué ponen en la mesa?
4. ¿Se olvidan de algo?
5. ¿Qué sacan del gabinete?
6. ¿Qué más ven en el gabinete?
7. ¿Qué hace el niño?

harina -
azúcar -
sal -
huevos -
horno -
salado –

8. ¿Qué hace la niña?
9. ¿ Dónde ponen las galletas?
10. ¿Qué hacen los niños ahora?
11. ¿Cómo saben las galletas?
12. ¿Qué había pasado?
13. ¿Qué harán con ellas?

Picture Story 36

Other Great Educational Materials by Lonnie Dai Zovi

www.Vibrante.com

Spanish ¡Alive! Whole Program – A pre-kindergarten through 2nd grade complete curriculum with 66 detailed lesson plans, stories, songs, activities, patterns, and pictures. An eclectic approach featuring modified TPRS. Set includes songbook/CD (below), story sheets, worksheets, and teacher's manual.

Spanish ¡Alive! (booklet & CD) – 15 simple children's songs including Hokey Pokey, Buenos Días, ¿Cómo te llamas? etc. Good for elementary classes and Spanish 1. Sold alone or part of set.

Español ¡Alegre! (booklet &CD) – 16 children's songs including songs about days, time, weather, school, food, etc. Good for all ages (also Spanish 1 & 2).

Cantos, Ritmos, Y Rimas – (Bk & CD) An innovative approach to learning Spanish vocabulary, syntax and grammar through chants set to Caribbean rhythms. Appropriate for all ages but mostly 5th – 12th grades.

Cantiques, Rhymes, Et Rimes – (Bk & CD) An innovative approach to learning French vocabulary, syntax, and grammar through Cajun, Zydeco, and Haitian rhythms. Appropriate for all ages but mostly 5th – 12th grades.

Canti, Ritmi e Rime is an exciting, revolutionary way of teaching and reinforcing Italian through chants set to catchy tunes or penetrating beats. The chants teach both thematic topics (family, weather, house, body, countries and more) and also grammatical points such as commands, prepositions, object pronouns, past tense with *essere/avere* and verb conjugations. No 5th through 12th grade Italian class should be without this CD/Book combination. The **Canti** set includes CD, scripts of the 21 songs, cloze exercises, and more.

Gesang, Rhythmen und Reime – (Bk & CD) An innovative approach to learning German vocabulary, syntax and grammar through all types of music, both modern and traditional. Appropriate for mostly 5th – 12th grades.

Cantos Calientes – (Bk & CD) More great chants for the classroom including por/para, preterite/imperfect, ser/estar and many subjunctive chants all set to Hispanic beats such as flamenco, salsa, andina, cumbia, vallenato and more.. Appropriate for Spanish 1-4.

Musical Arabic – An innovative CD/Book combination that pleasantly teaches and reinforces Modern Standard Arabic in a fun and non-threatening way. The book contains the scripts of the 22 lively chants, rhythms and songs (alphabet, birthday, family, countries, days, everyday expressions, possessives, simple verb conjugations, etc.) in both Arabic and phonetic (romanized) scripts for easier understanding by all students. There are many exercises that follow the lessons of the songs and also a picture glossary so that the learner may understand the songs without cumbersome translations. Good for all ages.

Rockin' Rhythms and Rhymes – (Workbook, Teacher's Guide & CD) A unique and innovative system of learning English through rhythmic recitations accompanied by music such as reggae, bluegrass, Irish jig, calypso, blues and much more. Grammar, vocabulary, and pronunciation stressed. Good for all ages.

Mariachi y Más – (Bk & CD) Indispensable music and workbook for intermediate, advanced, and bilingual classes. Mexico's 16 most beloved songs with scripts, cloze activities, worksheets, trivia, history, etc. Great AP tool.

Perfect Pics – Over 400 very appropriate blackline pictures for all language classes. Includes 112 verbs, 64 adjectives and hundreds more. Games, activities, and patterns are also provided. Great for games, quizzes, instruction and more. All levels and languages.

Practice with Pics – Workbook to stimulate simple oral or written expressions using pictures. Any language, any level especially low literacy students.

Perfect Picture Stories – 36 picture stories in 6 frames similar to the AP test with stimulus questions, vocabulary and oral comprehension questions in Spanish, French and English (German on request)

Expression Bingo - A set of 34 big bingo cards of 36 different common expressions including *What's your name?, How*

Accent on Art – Contains readings, exercises, maps, activities and more to teach/learn about 10 Mexican and Spanish artists; their lives, works and more. It is written in Spanish, which makes it applicable for the upper levels, or as a source book for teachers.

All may be purchased through major foreign language catalogs, or you may send for current prices directly from:

Vibrante Press
P.O. Box 51853
Albuquerque, New Mexico
87181-1853
505-298-4793
www.vibrante.com